A Treasury of

of

Children's
Poems

Published in 2001 by Brockhampton Press
20 Bloomsbury Street
London WC1B 3JH
a member of the Caxton Publishing Group

© 2001 Brockhampton Press

Designed and produced for Brockhampton Press
by Open Door Limited
Langham, Rutland

Compiled by Mandy Hancock
Illustration by Andrew Shepherd, Art Angle
Edited by Mary Morton
Typesetting by Jane and Richard Booth

Title: A Treasury of Children's Poems
ISBN: 1 84186 068 9

A Treasury
of
Children's
Poems

BROCKHAMPTON PRESS

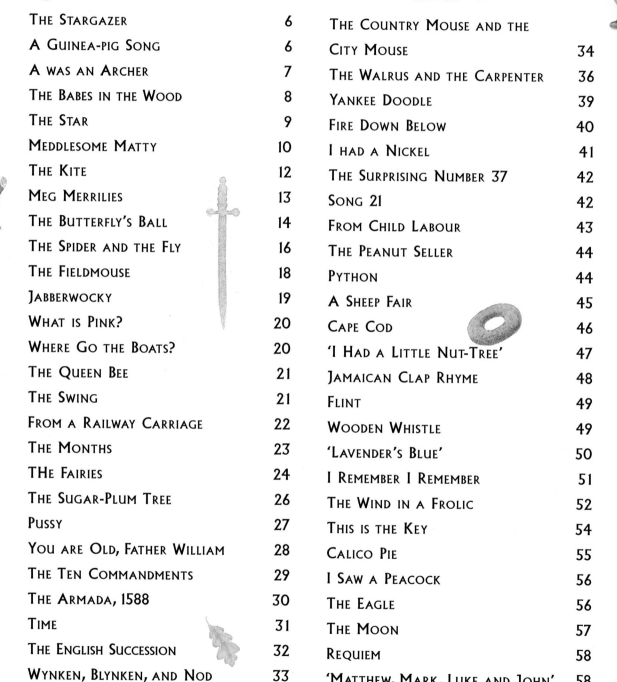

Contents

A Guinea-pig Song

There was a little guinea-pig,
Who, being little, was not big;
He always walked upon his feet,
And never fasted when he eat.

When from a place he run away,
He never at the place did stay;
And while he run, as I am told,
He ne'er stood still for young or old.

He often squeaked, and sometimes violent,
And when he squeaked, he ne'er was silent.
Though ne'er instructed by a cat,
He knew a mouse was not a rat.

One day, as I am certified,
He took a whim, and fairly died;
And as I am told by men of sense,
He never has been living since.

Anonymous

The Stargazer

A Stargazer out late at night,
With eyes and thoughts turned both upright,
Tumbled by chance into a well
(A dismal story this to tell);
He roared and sobbed, and roared again,
And cursed the 'Bear' and 'Charles's Wain.'

His woeful cries a neighbour brought,
Less learned, but wiser far in thought:
'My friend,' quoth he, 'you're much misled,
With stars to trouble thus your head;
Since you with these misfortunes meet,
For want of looking to your feet.'

Anonymous

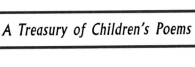

A was an Archer

A was an Archer, and shot at a frog,

B was a Blindman, and led by a dog.

C was a Cutpurse, and lived in disgrace,

D was a Drunkard, and had a red face.

E was an Eater, a glutton was he,

F was a Fighter, and fought with a flea.

G was a Giant, and pulled down a house,

H was a Hunter, and hunted a mouse.

I was an Ill man, and hated by all,

K was a Knave, and he robbed great and small.

L was a Liar, and told many lies,

M was a Madman, and beat out his eyes.

N was a Nobleman, nobly born,

O was an Ostler, and stole horses' corn.

P was a Pedlar, and sold many pins,

Q was a Quarreller, and broke both his shins.

R was a Rogue, and ran about town,

S was a Sailor, a man of renown.

T was a Tailor, and knavishly bent,

U was a Usurer, and took ten per cent.

W was a Writer, and money he earned,

X was one Xenophon, prudent and learn'd.

Y was a Yeoman, and worked for his bread,

Z was one Zeno the Great, but he's dead.

Ill man, bad man

The Babes in the Wood

My dear, do you know,
How a long time ago,
Two poor little children,

    Whose names I don't know,
    Were stolen away
    On a fine summer's day,
    And left in a wood,
    As I've heard people say?

Among the trees high,
Beneath the blue sky,
They plucked the bright flowers
And watched the birds fly;
Then on blackberries fed,
And strawberries red,
And when they were weary
'We'll go home,' they said.

And when it was night
So sad was their plight,
The sun it went down,
And the moon gave no light.
They sobbed and they sighed
    And they bitterly cried,
      And long before morning
        They lay down and died.

And when they were dead,
The robins so red
Brought strawberry leaves
And over them spread;
And all the day long,
The green branches among,
They'd prettily whistle,
And this was their song –
'Poor babes in the wood!
Sweet babes in the wood!
Oh the sad fate of
The babes in the wood!'

Anonymous

The Star

Twinkle, twinkle, little star,
How I wonder what you are!
Up above the world so high,
Like a diamond in the sky.

When the blazing sun is gone,
When he nothing shines upon,
Then you show your little light,
Twinkle, twinkle, all the night.

Then the traveller in the dark,
Thanks you for your tiny spark,
He could not see which way to go,
If you did not twinkle so.

In the dark blue sky you keep,
And often through my
curtains peep,
For you never
shut your eye,
Till the sun is
in the sky.

As your bright and tiny spark,
Lights the traveller in the dark –
Though I know not what you are,
Twinkle, twinkle, little star.

Jane Taylor 1783–1824

Meddlesome Matty

One ugly trick has often spoiled
The sweetest and the best;
Matilda, though a pleasant child,
One ugly trick possessed,
Which, like a cloud before the skies,
Hid all her better qualities.

Sometimes she'd lift the teapot lid,
To peep at what was in it;
Or tilt the kettle, if you did
But turn your back a minute.
In vain you told her not to touch,
Her trick of meddling
grew so much.

Her grandmamma
went out one day,
And by mistake she laid
Her spectacles and snuff-box gay
Too near the little maid;
'Ah well,' thought she, 'I'll try them on,
As soon as grandmamma is gone.'

Forthwith she placed upon her nose
The glasses large and wide;
And looking round, as I suppose,
The snuff-box too she spied:
'Oh, what a pretty box is this,
I'll open it,' said little Miss.

'I know that grandmamma would say,
"Don't meddle with it, dear,"
But then she's far enough away,
And no one else is near;
Besides, what can there be amiss
In opening such a box as this?'

So thumb and finger went to work
To move the stubborn lid,
And presently a mighty jerk
The mighty mischief did;
For all at once, ah! woeful case,
The snuff came puffing in her face.

Poor eyes, and nose, and mouth, and chin,
A dismal sight presented;
And as the snuff got further in,
Sincerely she repented.
In vain she ran about for ease,
She could do nothing else but sneeze.

She dashed the spectacles away,
To wipe her tingling eyes,
And as in twenty bits they lay,
Her grandmamma she spies.
'Heyday! and what's the matter now?'
Cried grandmamma, with lifted brow.

Matilda, smarting with the pain,
And tingling still, and sore,
Made many a promise to refrain
From meddling evermore;
And 'tis a fact, as I have heard,
She ever since has kept her word.

Ann Taylor 1782–1866

The Kite

My kite is three feet broad, and six
feet long;
The standard straight, the bender tough
and strong,
And to its milk-white breast five painted
stars belong.

Grand and majestic
soars my paper kite,
Through trackless skies
it takes its lofty flight:
Nor lark or eagle flies
to such a noble height.

As in the field I stand
and hold the twine,
Swift I unwind, to give it length of line,
Yet swifter it ascends, nor will to
earth incline.

Like a small speck, so high I see it sail,
I hear its pinions flutter in the gale,
And, like a flock of wild geese, sweeps its
flowing tail.

Adelaide O'Keefe
1776–1855

Meg Merrilies

Old Meg she was a gipsy,
And lived upon the moors;
Her bed it was the brown heath turf,
And her house was out of doors.
Her apples were swart blackberries,
Her currants, pods o' broom;
Her wine was dew of the wild white rose,
Her book a churchyard tomb.

Her brothers were the craggy hills,
Her sisters larchen trees;
Alone with her great family
She lived as she did please.
No breakfast had she many a morn,
No dinner many a noon,
And, 'stead of supper, she would stare
    Full hard against the moon.

But every morn, of
    woodbine fresh,
    She made her
    garlanding;
        And, every night, the
    dark glen yew
    She wove, and she would sing.
        And with her fingers, old and brown,
    She plaited mats of rushes,
    And gave them to the cottagers
    She met among the bushes.

Old Meg was brave as Margaret Queen,
And tall as an Amazon:
An old red blanket cloak she wore,
A chip-hat had she on.
God rest her aged bones somewhere –
She died full long agone!

John Keats 1795–1821

The Butterfly's Ball

Come take up your hats,
and away let us haste,
To the Butterfly's Ball,
and the Grasshopper's Feast.
The trumpeter Gadfly has
summoned the crew,
And the revels are now only
waiting for you.

On the smooth-shaven grass by
the side of a wood,
Beneath a broad oak which for
ages has stood,
See the children of earth and the
tenants of air,
For an evening's amusement
together repair.

And there came the Beetle,
so blind and so black,
Who carried the Emmet,
his friend, on his back.
And there came the Gnat,
and the Dragonfly too,
And all their relations, green,
orange, and blue.

And there came the Moth,
with her plumage of down,
And the Hornet, with jacket of
yellow and brown;
Who with him the Wasp,
his companion, did bring,
But they promised that evening,
to lay by their sting.

Then the sly little Dormouse crept
out of his hole,
And led to the feast his blind
cousin the Mole.
And the Snail, with his horns
peeping out of his shell,
Came, fatigued with the
distance,
the length of an ell.

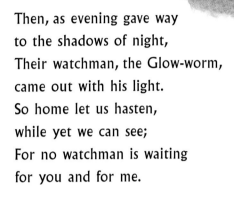

A mushroom their table,
and on it was laid
A water-dock leaf, which a
tablecloth made.
The viands were various,
to each of their taste,
And the Bee brought the honey
to sweeten the feast.

With steps most majestic
the Snail did advance,
And he promised the gazers a
minuet to dance;
But they all laughed so loud
that he drew in his head,
And went in his own little
chamber to bed.

Then, as evening gave way
to the shadows of night,
Their watchman, the Glow-worm,
came out with his light.
So home let us hasten,
while yet we can see;
For no watchman is waiting
for you and for me.

William Roscoe 1753–1831

The Spider and the Fly

'Will you walk into my parlour?'
said the Spider to the Fly,
'Tis the prettiest little parlour that ever you
did spy;
The way into my parlour is up a
winding stair,
And I have many curious things to
show when you are there.'
'Oh no, no, no,' said the little Fly,
'To ask me is in vain,
For who goes up your winding stair can
ne'er come down again.'

'I'm sure you must be weary, dear, with
soaring up so high;
Will you rest upon my little bed?'
said the Spider to the Fly.
'There are pretty curtains drawn around,
the sheets are fine and thin;
And if you like to rest awhile, I'll snugly
tuck you in!'
'Oh no, no, no,' said the little Fly,
'for I've often heard it said,
They never, never wake again,
who sleep upon your bed!'

Said the cunning Spider to the Fly,
'Dear friend, what can I do,
To prove the warm affection
I've always felt for you?
I have within my pantry good store of all
that's nice;
I'm sure you're very welcome – will you
please to take a slice?'
'Oh no, no, no,' said the little Fly,
'kind sir, that cannot be,
I've heard what's in your pantry, and I do
not wish to see.'

'Sweet creature,' said the Spider,
 'you're witty and you're wise;
How handsome are your gauzy wings,
how brilliant are your eyes!
I have a little looking-glass upon my
parlour shelf,
If you'll step in a moment, dear, you shall
behold yourself.'
'I thank you gentle sir,' she said,
'for what you're pleased to say,
And bidding you good morning now,
I'll call another day.'

The Spider turned him round
about, and went into his den,
For well he knew the silly Fly
would soon come back again;
So he wove a subtle web, in a
little corner sly,
And set his table ready, to dine upon the Fly.

Then he came out
to his door again,
and merrily did sing:
'Come hither, hither,
pretty Fly, with the
pearl and silver wing;
Your robes are green
and purple –
there's a crest upon
your head;
Your eyes are like the diamond bright,
but mine are dull as lead.'
Alas, alas! how very soon this silly little Fly,
Hearing his wily, flattering words, came
slowly flitting by;
With buzzing wings she hung aloft, then
near and nearer drew,
Thinking only of her brilliant eyes, and
green and purple hue;
Thinking only of her crested head – poor
foolish thing! At last,
Up jumped the cunning Spider,
and fiercely held her fast.
He dragged her up his winding stair,
   into his dismal den,
      Within his little parlour – but she
         ne'er came out again!

Mary Howitt 1799–1888

The Fieldmouse

Where the acorn tumbles down,
Where the ash tree sheds its berry,
With your fur so soft and brown,
With your eye so round and merry,
Scarcely moving the long grass,
Fieldmouse, I can see you pass.

Little thing, in what dark den,
Lie you all the winter sleeping?
Till warm weather comes again,
Then once more I see you peeping
Round about the tall tree roots,
Nibbling at their fallen fruits.

Fieldmouse, fieldmouse, do not go,
Where the farmer stacks his treasure,
Find the nut that falls below,
Eat the acorn at your pleasure,
But you must not steal the grain
He has stacked with so much pain.

Make your hole where mosses spring,
Underneath the tall oak's shadow,
Pretty, quiet, harmless thing,
Play about the sunny meadow.
Keep away from corn and house,
None will harm you, little mouse.

Cecil Frances Alexander 1818–1895

Jabberwocky

'Twas brillig, and the slithy toves
Did gyre and gimble in the wabe:
All mimsy were the borogoves,
And the mome raths outgrabe.

'Beware the Jabberwock, my son!
The jaws that bite, the claws that catch!
Beware the Jubjub bird, and shun
The frumious Bandersnatch!'

He took his vorpal sword in hand:
Long time the manxome foe he sought –
So rested he by the Tumtum tree,
And stood awhile in thought.

And as in uffish thought he stood
The Jabberwock, with eyes of flame,
Came whiffling through the tulgey wood,
And burbled as it came!

One, two! One, two! And through and
through
The vorpal blade went snicker-snack!
He left it dead, and with its head
He went galumphing back.

'And hast thou slain the Jabberwock?
Come to my arms, my beamish boy!
O frabjous day! Callooh! Callay!'
He chortled in his joy.

'Twas brillig, and the slithy toves
Did gyre and gimble in the wabe:
All mimsy were the borogoves,
And the mome raths outgrabe.

Lewis Carroll 1832–1898

What is Pink?

What is pink? A rose is pink
By the fountain's brink.
What is red? A poppy's red
In its barley bed.
What is blue? The sky is blue
Where the clouds float through.
What is white? A swan is white
Sailing in the light.
What is yellow? Pears are yellow
Rich and ripe and mellow.
What is green? The grass is green
With small flowers between.
What is violet? Clouds are violet
In the summer twilight.
What is orange?
Why, an orange,
Just an orange!

Anonymous

Where Go the Boats?

Dark brown is the river,
Golden is the sand.
It flows along for ever,
With trees on either hand.

Green leaves a-floating,
Castles of the foam,
Boats of mine a-boating –
Where will all come home?

On goes the river,
And out past the mill,
Away down the valley,
Away down the hill.

Away down the river,
A hundred miles or more,
Other little children
Shall bring my boats ashore.

Cecil Frances Alexander 1818–1895

The Queen Bee

When I was in the garden,
I saw a great Queen Bee;
She was the very largest one
That I did ever see.
She wore a shiny helmet
And a lovely velvet gown,
But I was rather sad, because
She didn't wear a crown.

Mary K. Robinson

The Swing

How do you like to go up in a swing,
Up in the air so blue?
Oh, I do think it the pleasantest thing
Ever a child can do!

Up in the air and over the wall,
Till I can see so wide,
Rivers and trees and cattle and all
Over the countryside –

Till I look down on the garden green,
Down on the roof so brown –
Up in the air I go flying again,
Up in the air and down.

Robert Louis Stevenson 1850–1894

From a Railway Carriage

Faster than fairies, faster than witches,
Bridges and houses, hedges and ditches;
And charging along like troops in a battle,
All through the meadows the horses and
cattle:

All of the sights of the hill and the plain
Fly as thick as driving rain;
And ever again, in the wink of an eye,
Painted stations whistle by.

Here is a child who clambers and scrambles,
All by himself and gathering brambles;

Here is a tramp who stands and gazes;
And there is the green for stringing the
daisies!

Here is a cart run away in the road
Lumping along with man and load;
And here is a mill, and there is a river:
Each a glimpse and gone forever!

Robert Louis Stevenson 1850-1894

The Months

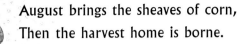

January brings the snow,
Makes our feet and fingers glow.

February brings the rain,
Thaws the frozen lake again.

March brings breezes loud and shrill,
Stirs the dancing daffodil.

April brings the primrose sweet,
Scatters daisies at our feet.

May brings flocks of pretty lambs,
Skipping by their fleecy dams.

August brings the sheaves of corn,
Then the harvest home is borne.

Warm September brings
the fruit,
Sportsmen then begin to shoot.

Fresh October brings the pheasant,
Then to gather nuts is pleasant.

Dull November brings the blast,
Then the leaves are whirling fast.

June brings tulips, lilies, roses,
Fills the children's hands with posies.

Hot July brings cooling showers,
Apricots and gillyflowers.

Chill December brings the sleet,
Blazing fire, and Christmas treat.

Sara Coleridge 1802–1852

The Fairies

Up the airy mountain,
Down the rushy glen,
We daren't go a-hunting
For fear of little men;
Wee folk, good folk,
Trooping all together;
Green jacket, red cap,
And white owl's feather!

Down along the rocky shore
Some make their home,
They live on crispy pancakes
Of yellow tide-foam;
Some in the reeds
Of the black mountain-lake,
With frogs for their watchdogs,
All night awake.

High on the hill-top
The old king sits;
He is now so old and grey
He's nigh lost his wits.
With a bridge of white mist
Columbkill he crosses,
On his stately journeys
From Slieveleague to Rosses;
Or going up with music
On cold starry nights,
To sup with the Queen
Of the gay Northern Lights.

They stole little Bridget
For seven years long;
When she came down again
Her friends were all gone.
They took her lightly back,
Between the night and morrow,
They thought that she was fast asleep,
But she was dead with sorrow.
They have kept her ever since
Deep within the lake,
On a bed of flag-leaves,
Watching till she wake.

Up the airy mountain,
Down the rushy glen,
We daren't go a-hunting
For fear of little men;
Wee folk, good folk,
Trooping all together;
Green jacket, red cap,
And white owl's feather!

William Allingham 1824–1889

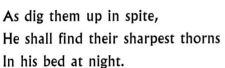

By the craggy hillside,
Through the mosses bare,
They have planted thorn trees
For pleasure here and there.
Is any man so daring

As dig them up in spite,
He shall find their sharpest thorns
In his bed at night.

The Sugar-Plum Tree

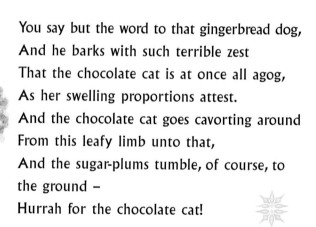

Have you ever heard of the Sugar-Plum Tree?
'Tis a marvel of great renown!
It blooms on the shore of the Lollipop sea
In the garden of Shut-Eye Town;
The fruit that it bears is so wondrously
sweet (As those who have tasted it say)
That good little children have only to eat
Of that fruit to be happy next day.

When you've got to the tree, you would
have a hard time
To capture the fruit which I sing;
The tree is so tall that no person could climb
To the boughs where the sugar-plums swing.
But up in that tree sits a chocolate cat,
And a gingerbread dog prowls below –
And this is the way you contrive to get at
Those sugar-plums tempting you so:

You say but the word to that gingerbread dog,
And he barks with such terrible zest
That the chocolate cat is at once all agog,
As her swelling proportions attest.
And the chocolate cat goes cavorting around
From this leafy limb unto that,
And the sugar-plums tumble, of course, to
the ground –
Hurrah for the chocolate cat!

There are marshmallows, gumdrops, and
peppermint canes,
With stripings of scarlet or gold,
And you carry away of the treasure that rains
As much as your apron can hold!
So come, little child, cuddle closer to me
In your dainty white nightcap and gown,
And I'll rock you away to that Sugar-Plum Tree
In the garden of Shut-Eye Town.

Eugene Field 1850–1895

Pussy

I like little pussy, her coat is so warm;
And if I don't hurt her, she'll do me
no harm.
So I'll not pull her tail, nor drive her away,
But pussy and I very gently will play.
She shall sit by my side, and I'll give her
some food;
And she'll love me because I am gentle
and good.

I'll pat pretty pussy, and then she will purr;
And thus show her thanks for my
kindness to her.
But I'll not pinch her ears, nor tread on
her paw,
Lest I should provoke her to use her
sharp claw.
I never will vex her, nor make her displeased
For pussy don't like to be worried
and teased.

Anonymous c. 1830

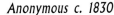

You are Old, Father William

'You are old, Father
William,' the young
man said,
'And your hair has
become very white;
And yet you incessantly
stand on your head –
Do you think, at your
age, it is right?'

'In my youth,' Father
William replied to his son,
'I feared it might injure the brain;
But, now that I'm perfectly sure I have none,
Why, I do it again and again.'

'You are old,' said the youth,
'as I mentioned before,
And have grown most
uncommonly fat;
Yet you turned a back-
somersault in at the door –
Pray, what is the reason
of that?'

'In my youth,' said the sage, as he shook
his grey locks,
'I kept all my limbs very supple
By the use of this ointment – one shilling
the box –
Allow me to sell you a couple?'

'You are old,' said the youth, 'and your
jaws are too weak
For anything tougher than suet;
Yet you finished the goose, with the
bones and the beak –
Pray, how did you manage to do it?'

'In my youth,' said his father, 'I
took to the law,
And argued each case with my wife;
And the muscular strength, which
it gave to my jaw,
Has lasted the rest of my life.'

'You are old,' said the youth, 'one would
hardly suppose
That your eye was as steady as ever;
Yet you balanced an eel on the
end of your nose –
What made you so awfully clever?'

'I have answered three questions,
and that is enough,'
Said his father;
'Don't give yourself airs!
Do you think I can listen all day
to such stuff?
Be off, or I'll kick you
downstairs!'

Lewis Carroll 1832–1898

The Ten Commandments

I. Have thou no other gods but me,
II. And to no image bow thy knee.
III. Take not the name of God in vain:
IV. The sabbath day do not profane.
V. Honour thy father and mother too;
VI. And see that thou no murder do.
VII. Abstain from words and deeds unclean;
VIII. Nor steal, though thou art poor
and mean.

IX. Bear not false witness,
shun that blot;
X. What is thy
neighbour's covet not.

These laws, O Lord, write in my heart,
that I,
May in thy faithful service live and die.

Anonymous

The Armada, 1588

Our little fleet in July first,
Their mighty fleet did view:
She came but with a softly course,
Though winds behind her blew.
Her front much like the moon was crook'd,
(The horns seven miles asunder)
   Her masts like stately towers looked,
      The ocean groaning under.
      And now, behold,
        they were at hand,
          Daring our English borders,
          Making full sure to
          bring our land
        Under their Spanish orders.

But God above,
laughing to scorn
Their wicked wile, and wealth,
To his annointed raised an horn
Of hope and saving health.
Prince, prophets, people, jointly cried
To Christ alone for aid;
Whose power invincible was tried
With banner all displayed.
That noble Drake drove on apace,
And made the Spaniard dive;
And Hawkins followed hard the chase
(As hawk doth covey drive).

With these, well furbished Frobisher
Their navy did assail:
All at her back did thunder her
And swept away her tail.
Those were the worthies three, which first
(Next to their Admiral)
Ventured the hostile ranks to burst
(Spite of their Don Recalde);
And many more of great renown
Did bravely play their part,
In skill and valour putting down
The Spanish strength and art.
But why do I record the men,
That fought with such as braved us?
I said, and so I say again,
It was the Lord that saved us.

John Wilson 1785–1854

30

Time

Time's a hand's-breadth; 'tis a tale;
'Tis a vessel under sail;
'Tis an eagle in its way,
Darting down upon its prey;
'Tis an arrow in its flight,
Mocking the pursuing sight;
'Tis a short-lived fading flower;
'Tis a rainbow on a shower;
'Tis a momentary ray,

Smiling in a winter's day;
'Tis a torrent's rushing stream;
'Tis a shadow; 'tis a dream;
'Tis the closing watch of night,
Dying at the rising light;
'Tis a bubble; 'tis a sigh:
Be prepared, O Man! to die.

John Huddlestone Wynne 1743–1788

The English Succession

The Norman Conquest all historians fix
To the year of Christ, one thousand
sixty-six.
Two Wills, one Henry, Stephen, Kings
are reckoned;
    Then rose Plantagenet in
    Henry second.
    First Richard, John, third
    Henry, Edwards three,
    And second Richard
    in one line we see.
    Fourth, fifth, and sixth Lancastrian
Henrys reign;
Then Yorkist Edwards two, and Richard slain.
Next Tudor comes in seventh Henry's right,
Who the red rose engrafted on the white.
Eighth Henry, Edward sixth, first Mary, Bess;
Then Scottish Stuart's right the peers
confess.

James, double Charles, a second James
expelled;
With Mary, Will; then Anne the sceptre held.
Last, Brunswick's issue has two Georges given;
Late may the second pass from earth to
heaven!

John Marchant

Wynken, Blynken, and Nod

All night long their nets they threw
To the stars in the twinkling foam –
Then down from the skies came the
wooden shoe,
Bringing the fishermen home;
'Twas all so pretty a sail it seemed
As if it could not be,
And some folks thought 'twas a dream
they'd dreamed
Of sailing that beautiful sea –
But I shall name you the fishermen three:
Wynken,
Blynken,
And Nod.

Wynken and Blynken are two little eyes,
And Nod is a little head,
And the wooden shoe that sailed the skies
Is the wee one's trundle-bed.
So shut your eyes while mother sings
Of wonderful things that be,
And you shall see the beautiful things
As you rock in the misty sea,
Where the old shoe rocked the fishermen
three:
Wynken,
Blynken,
And Nod.

Eugene Field 1850–1895

The Country Mouse and the City Mouse

In a snug little cot lived a fat little mouse,
Who enjoyed, unmolested, the range of the
house;
With plain food content, she would
breakfast on cheese,
She dined upon bacon, and supped on grey peas.

A friend from the town to the cottage
did stray,
And he said he was come a short visit
to pay;
So the mouse spread her table as gay as
you please,
And brought the nice bacon and charming
grey peas.

The visitor frowned, and he thought to
be witty:
Cried he, 'You must know, I am come from
the city,
Where we all should be shocked at
provisions like these,
For we never eat bacon and horrid grey peas.

To town come with me, I will give
you a treat:
Some excellent food, most delightful to eat.
With me you shall feast just as long as
you please;
Come, leave this fat bacon and shocking
grey peas.'

This kind invitation she could not refuse,
And the city mouse wished not a moment
to lose;
Reluctant she quitted the fields and
the trees,
The delicious fat bacon and charming
grey peas.

They slily crept under a gay parlour door,
Where a feast had been given the
evening before;
And it must be confessed they on
dainties did seize,
far better than bacon, or even grey peas.

Here were custard and trifle, and
cheesecakes good store,
Nice sweetmeats and jellies, and twenty
things more;
All that art had invented the palate
to please,
Except some fat bacon and smoking
grey peas.

They were nicely regaling, when into
the room
Came the dog and the cat, and the maid
with a broom:
They jumped in a custard both up to
their knees;
The country mouse sighed for her bacon
and peas.

Cried she to her friend, 'Get me safely away,
I can venture no longer in London to stay;
For if oft you receive interruptions like these,
Give me my nice bacon and charming
grey peas.

'Your living is splendid and gay, to be sure,
But the dread of disturbance you ever endure;
I taste true delight in contentment and ease,
And I feast on fat bacon and charming
grey peas.'

Richard Scrafton Sharpe 1775–1852

The Walrus and the Carpenter
Were walking close at hand;
They wept like anything to see
Such quantities of sand:
'If this were only cleared away,'
They said, 'it would be grand!'

'If seven maids with seven mops
Swept it for half a year,
Do you suppose,' the Walrus said,
'That they could get it clear?'
'I doubt it,' said the Carpenter,
And shed a bitter tear.

The Walrus and the Carpenter

The sun was shining on the sea,
Shining with all his might:
He did his very best to make
The billows smooth and bright –
And this was odd, because it was
The middle of the night.

The moon was shining sulkily,
Because she thought the sun
Had got no business to be there
After the day was done –
'It's very rude of him,' she said,
'To come and spoil the fun!'

The sea was wet as wet could be,
The sands were dry as dry.
You could not see a cloud, because
No cloud was in the sky:
No birds were flying overhead –
There were no birds to fly.

'O Oysters, come and walk
   with us!'
   The Walrus did beseech.
  'A pleasant walk, a pleasant talk,
   Along the briny beach:
We cannot do with more than four,
To give a hand to each.'

The eldest Oyster looked at him,
But never a word he said:
The eldest Oyster winked his eye,
And shook his heavy head –
Meaning to say he did not choose
To leave his oyster-bed.

But four young Oysters hurried up,
All eager for the treat:
Their coats were brushed, their faces
washed,
Their shoes were clean and neat –
And this was odd, because, you know,
They hadn't any feet.

Four other Oysters followed them,
And yet another four;
And thick and fast they came at last,
And more, and more, and more –
All hopping through the frothy waves,
And scrambling to the shore.

The Walrus and the Carpenter
Walked on a mile or so,
And then they rested on a rock
Conveniently low:
And all the little Oysters stood
And waited in a row.

'The time has come,' the Walrus said,
'To talk of many things:
Of shoes – and ships – and sealing wax –
Of cabbages – and kings –
And why the sea is boiling hot –
And whether pigs have wings.'

'But wait a bit,' the Oysters cried,
'Before we have our chat;
For some of us are out of breath,
And all of us are fat!'
'No hurry!' said the Carpenter.
They thanked him much for that.

'A loaf of bread,' the Walrus said,
'Is what we chiefly need:
Pepper and vinegar besides
Are very good indeed –
Now if you're ready, Oysters dear,
We can begin to feed.'

'But not on us!' the Oysters cried,
Turning a little blue.
'After such a kindness, that would be
A dismal thing to do!'
'The night is fine,' the Walrus said,
'Do you admire the view?'

'It was so kind of you to come!
And you are very nice!'
The Carpenter said nothing but
'Cut us another slice:
I wish you were not quite so deaf –
I've had to ask you twice!'

'It seems a shame,' the Walrus said,
'To play them such a trick,
After we've brought them out so far,
And made them trot so quick!'
The Carpenter said nothing but
'The butter's spread too thick!'

'I weep for you,' the Walrus said:
'I deeply sympathize.'
With sobs and tears he sorted out
Those of the largest size,
Holding his pocket-handkerchief
Before his streaming eyes.

'O Oysters,' said the Carpenter,
'You've had a pleasant run!
Shall we be trotting home again?'
But answer came there none –
And this was scarcely odd, because
They'd eaten every one.

Lewis Carroll 1832–1898

Yankee Doodle

Yankee Doodle went to town,
He rode a little pony,
He stuck a feather in his hat
And called it macaroni.
Yankee Doodle fa, so, la,
Yankee Doodle dandy.
Yankee Doodle fa, so, la,
Buttermilk and brandy.

Yankee Doodle went to town
To buy a pair of trousers,
He swore he could
not see the town
For so many houses.
Yankee Doodle
fa, so, la,
Yankee Doodle dandy.
Yankee Doodle
fa, so, la,
Buttermilk and brandy.

Traditional

Fire Down Below

There is fire in the lower hold,
There's fire down below,
Fire in the main well,
The captain didn't know.

There is fire in the forepeek,
Fire in the main,
Fire in the windlass,
Fire in the chain.

There is fire in the foretop,
Fire down below,
Fire in the chain-plates,
The boats'ain didn't know.

There is fire up aloft,
There is fire down below,
Fire in the galley,
The cook he didn't know.

Anonymous

I had a Nickel

I had a nickel and I walked around
the block.
I walked right into a baker shop.
I took two doughnuts right out of
the grease;
I handed the lady my five cent piece.
She looked at the nickel
and she looked at me,

And said, 'This money's no good to me,
There's a hole in the nickel, and it goes
right through.'
Says I, 'There's a hole in the doughnut, too.'

Anonymous

Song 21

The tongue of the Lightning flashes along the top of the clouds. . .
Making them shine like red ochre, flashing along the yellow clouds. . .
The Lightning Snake moving its tail, rearing its head quickly from its hole. . .
Great Lightning Snake, flashing along the clouds:
Coming out from its camp, striking the clouds. . .
The Snake, salt-water creature making thin streaks of lightning.
The tongue of the Lightning flashes along the top of the clouds. . .
Making them shine like red ochre, flashing along the yellow clouds. . .

Australian Aborigine Poem

The Surprising Number 37

The number 37 has a special magic to it.
If you multiply 37 by 3, you get 111.
If you multiply 37 by 6, you get 222.
If you multiply 37 by 9, you get 333.
If you multiply 37 by 12, you get 444.
If you multiply 37 by 15, you get 555.
If you multiply 37 by 18, you get 666.
If you multiply 37 by 21, you get 777.
If you multiply 37 by 24, you get 888.
If you multiply 37 by 27, you get 999.

Anonymous

For all day the wheels are
droning, turning;
Their wind comes in our faces,
Till our hearts turn, our heads
with pulses burning,
And the walls turn in their places:
Turns the sky in the high window, blank
and reeling,
Turns the long light that drops adown
the wall,
Turn the black flies that crawl along
the ceiling:
All are turning, all the day, and we with all.
And all day, the iron wheels are droning,
And sometimes we could pray,
'O ye wheels' (breaking out in a mad moaning)
'Stop! be silent for to-day!'

Elizabeth Barrett Browning
1806–1861

From Child Labour

'For oh,' say the children, 'we are weary
And we cannot run or leap;
If we cared for any meadows, it were merely
To drop down in them and sleep.
Our knees tremble sorely in the stooping,
We fall upon our faces, trying to go;
And underneath our heavy eyelids drooping
The reddest flower would look as pale
as snow.
For, all day, we drag our burden tiring
Through the coal-dark, underground;
Or, all day, we drive the wheels of iron
In the factories, round and round.

Python

Swaggering prince
Giant among snakes.
They say the python has no house.
I heard it a long time ago
And I laughed and laughed and laughed.
For who owns the ground under the lemon
grass?
Who owns the ground under the elephant
grass?
Who owns the swamp – father of rivers?
Who owns the stagnant pool – father of
waters?

Because they never walk hand in hand
People say that snakes only walk singly.
But just imagine.
Suppose the viper walks in front
The green mamba follows
And the python creeps rumbling behind –
Who will be brave enough
To wait for them?

Yoruba Poem

The Peanut Seller

Peanuts!
Two bags for five!

They brush your teeth.
They curl your hair;
They make you feel
Like a millionaire!

Peanuts!
Two bags for five!

New Orleans Street Cry

A Sheep Fair

The day arrives of the autumn fair,
And torrents fall,
Though sheep in throngs are gathered there,
Ten thousand all,
Sodden, with hurdles round them reared:
And, lot by lot, the pens are cleared,
And the auctioneer wrings out his beard,
And wipes his book, bedrenched and smeared,
And rakes the rain from his face with the
      edge of his hand,
      As torrents fall.

      The wool of the ewes is like
      a sponge
      With the daylong rain:
Jammed tight, to turn, or lie, or lunge,
They strive in vain.

Their horns are soft as finger-nails,
Their shepherds reek against the rails,
The tied-dogs soak with tucked-in tails,
The buyers' hat brims fill like pails,
Which spill small cascades when they shift
their stand
In the daylong rain.

Thomas Hardy
1840–1928

Cape Cod

Cape Cod girls have no combs
They comb their hair with codfish bones

Cape Cod boys have no sleds
They slide down dunes on codfish heads

Cape Cod doctors have no pills
They give their patients codfish gills

Cape Cod cats have no tails
They lost them in the sou'east gales.

Anonymous

'I Had a Little Nut-Tree'

I had a little nut-tree,
Nothing would it bear
But a silver nutmeg
And a golden pear.

The King of Spain's daughter
Came to visit me,
All for the sake
Of my little nut-tree.

I skipped over ocean,
I danced over sea;
And all the birds in the air
Couldn't catch me!

Traditional

Jamaican Clap Rhyme

Where your mamma gone?
She gone down town.

She take any money?
She take ten pound.

When your mamma come back,
what she gonna bring back?

Hats and frocks and
shoes and socks.

Anonymous

Wooden Whistle

I bought
a wooden
whistle,
but it
wooden
whistle.
I bought
a steel
whistle,
but it
steel
wooden
whistle.
So
I bought
a tin
whistle.
And now
I tin
whistle!

Flint

An emerald is as green as grass,
A ruby red as blood;
A sapphire shines as blue as heaven;
A flint lies in the mud.

A diamond is a brilliant stone,
To catch the world's desire;
An opal holds a fiery spark;
But a flint holds fire.

Christina Rossetti 1830–1894

Anonymous

'Lavender's Blue'

Lavender's blue, dilly dilly:
lavender's green;
When I am King, dilly dilly,
you shall be Queen.
Who told you that, dilly dilly,
who told you so?
'Twas my own heart,
dilly dilly, that told me so.

Call up your men, dilly dilly,
set them to work;
Some to the plough, dilly dilly,
some to the cart;
Some to make hay, dilly dilly,
some to thresh corn,
While you and I, dilly dilly,
keep ourselves warm.

If I should die, dilly dilly,
as well may hap,
Bury me deep, dilly dilly,
under the tap;
Under the tap, dilly dilly,
I'll tell you why,
That I may drink, dilly dilly,
when I am dry.

Traditional

I remember I remember

I remember, I remember
The house where I was born,
The little window where the sun
Came peeping in at morn;
He never came a wink to soon
Nor brought too long a day,
But now, I often wish the night
Had borne my breath away.

I remember, I remember
The roses, red and white,
The violets, and lily-cups,
Those flowers made of light!
The lilacs where the robin built,
and where my brother set
The laburnum on his birthday –
The tree is living yet!

I remember, I remember
Where I was used to swing;
And thought the air must rush as fresh
To swallows on the wing:
My spirit flew in feathers then,
That is so heavy now,
And summer pools could hardly cool
The fever on my brow!

I remember, I remember
The fir trees dark and high;
I used to think their slender tops
Were close against the sky:
It was a childish ignorance,
But now 'tis little joy
To know I'm farther
off from Heav'n
Than when I was a boy.

Thomas Hood
1799–1845

The Wind in a Frolic

The wind one morning sprung up from sleep,
Saying, 'Now for a frolic! now for a leap!
Now for a mad-cap, galloping chase!
I'll make a commotion in every place!'
So it swept with a bustle right through a
great town,
Creaking the signs, and scattering down
Shutters; and whisking, with merciless squalls,
Old women's bonnets and gingerbread stalls.
There never was heard a much lustier shout,

As the apples and oranges trundled about;
And the urchins, that stand with their
thievish eyes
For ever on watch, ran off each with a prize.
Then away to the field it went blustering
and humming,
And the cattle all wondered whatever was
coming;
It plucked by their tails the grave, matronly
cows,
And tossed the colts' manes all about their
brows,
And offended at such a familiar salute,
They all turned their backs, and stood
sullenly mute.

So on it went, capering and playing its
pranks:
Whistling with reeds on the broad river's
banks;
Puffing the birds as they sat on the spray,
Or the traveller grave on the king's highway.
It was not too nice to hustle the bags
Of the beggar, and flutter his dirty rags:
'Twas so bold that it feared not to play its
joke
With the doctor's wig, or the gentleman's
cloak.
Through the forest it roared, and cried gaily,
'Now,
You sturdy old oaks, I'll make you bow!'
And it made them bow without more ado,
Or it cracked their great branches through
and through.

With his hat in a pool, and his shoe in the mud.
There was a poor man, hoary and old,
Cutting the heath on the open wold -
The strokes of his bill were faint and few,
Ere this frolicsome wind upon him blew;
But behind him, before him, about him it came,
And the breath seemed gone from his feeble frame;
So he sat him down with a muttering tone,
Saying, 'Plague on the wind! was the like ever known?
But nowadays every wind that blows
Tells one how weak an old man grows!'

Then it rushed like a monster on cottage and farm,
Striking their dwellers with sudden alarm;
And they ran out like bees in a midsummer swarm.
There were dames with their 'kerchiefs tied over their caps,
To see if their poultry were free from mishaps;
The turkeys they gobbled, the geese screamed aloud,
And the hens crept to roost in a terrified crowd;
There was rearing of ladders, and logs laying on
Where the thatch from the roof threatened soon to be gone.

But the wind had passed on, and had met in a lane,
With a schoolboy, who panted and struggled in vain;
For it tossed him, and twirled him, then passed, and he stood,

But away went the wind in its holiday glee;
And now it was far on the billowy sea,
And the lordly ships felt its staggering blow,
And the little boats darted to and fro.
But lo! it was night, and it sank to rest,
On the sea-bird's rock, in the gleaming west,
Laughing to think, in its fearful fun,
How little of mischief it had done.

William Howitt 1792–1879

This is the Key

This is the Key of the Kingdom
In that Kingdom is a city;
In that city is a town;
In that town there is a street;
In that street there winds a lane;
In that lane there is a yard;
In that yard there is a house;
In that house there waits a room;
In that room an empty bed;
And on that bed a basket –
A Basket of Sweet Flowers
Of Flowers, of Flowers;
A Basket of Sweet Flowers.

Flowers in a Basket;
basket on the bed;
Bed in the chamber;
Chamber in the house;
House in the weedy yard;
Yard in the winding lane;
Lane in the broad street;
Street in the high town;
Town in the city;
City in the Kingdom –
This is the Key of the Kingdom.
Of the Kingdom this is the Key.

Traditional

Calico Pie

Calico Pie,
The little Birds fly
Down to their calico tree,
Their wings were blue,
And they sang 'Tilly-loo!'
Till away they flew –
And they never came back to me!
They never came back!
They never came back!
They never came back to me!

Calico Jam,
The little Fish swam
Over the syllabub sea,
He took off his hat,
To the Sole and the Sprat,
And the Willeby-wat –
But he never came back to me!
He never came back!
He never came back!
He never came back to me!

Calico Ban,
The little Mice ran,
To be ready in time for tea,
Flippity flup,
They drank it all up,
And danced in the cup –
But they never came back to me!
They never came back!
They never came back!
They never came back to me!

Calico Drum,
The Grasshoppers come,
The Butterfly, Beetle and Bee,
Over the ground,
Around and round,
With a hop and a bound –
But they never came back!
They never came back!
They never came back!
They never came back to me!

Edward Lear 1812–1888

The Eagle

He clasps the crag with crooked hands;
Close to the sun in lonely lands,
Ringed with the azure world, he stands.

The wrinkled sea beneath him crawls;
He watches from his mountain walls,
And like a thunderbolt he falls.

Alfred, Lord Tennyson
1809–1892

I Saw a Peacock

I saw a Peacock with a fiery tail,
I saw a blazing Comet drop down hail,
I saw a Cloud with ivy circled round,
I saw a sturdy Oak creep on the ground,
I saw a Pismire swallow up a whale,
I saw a raging Sea brim full of ale,
I saw a Venice Glass sixteen foot deep,
I saw a Well full of men's tears that weep,
I saw their Eyes all in flame of fire,
I saw a House as big as the moon and higher
I saw the Sun even in the midst of night,
I saw the Man that saw this wondrous sight.

Traditional

The Moon

The moon has a face
like the clock in the hall;
She shines on thieves
on the garden wall,
On streets and fields
and harbour quays,
And birdies asleep
in the forks of trees.

The squalling cat
and the squeaking mouse,
The howling dog
by the door of the house,
The bat that lies
in bed at noon,
All love to be out
     by the light of the moon.

       But all the things
        that belong to the day
        Cuddle to sleep
        to be out of her way;
       And flowers and children
close their eyes
Till up in the morning
the sun shall arise.

Robert Louis Stevenson 1850–1894

'Matthew, Mark, Luke and John'

Matthew, Mark, Luke and John,
Bless the bed that I lie on.
Before I lay me down to sleep
I give my soul to Christ to keep.
Four corners to my bed,
Four angels there aspread,
Two to foot, and two to head,
And four to carry me when I'm dead.
I go by sea, I go by land,
The Lord made me with His right hand.
If any danger come to me,
Sweet Jesus Christ deliver me.
He's the branch and I'm the flower,
Pray God send me a happy hour,
And if I die before I wake,
I pray that Christ my soul will take.

Traditional

Requiem

Under the wide and starry sky
Dig the grave and let me lie:
Glad did I live and gladly die,
And I laid me down with a will.

This is the verse you grave for me
Here he lies where he longed to be;
Home is the sailor, home from the sea,
And the hunter home from the hill.

Robert Louis Stevenson 1850–1894

In the Bleak Midwinter

In the bleak midwinter,
frosty wind made moan,
earth stood hard as iron,
Water like a stone;
Snow had fallen, snow on snow,
Snow on snow,
In the bleak midwinter,
Long ago.

What can I give him?
Poor as I am?
If I were a shepherd,
I would bring a lamb;
If I were a wise man,
I would do my part;
Yet what I can I give him –
Give my heart.

Christina Rossetti 1830–1894

The Owl and the Pussy-cat

The Owl and the Pussy-cat went to sea
In a beautiful pea-green boat.
They took some honey, and plenty
of money
Wrapped up in a five-pound note.
The Owl looked up to the stars above,
And sang to a small guitar,
'O lovely Pussy! O Pussy, my love,
What a beautiful Pussy you are,
  You are,
  You are!
What a beautiful Pussy you are!'

Pussy said to the Owl, 'You elegant fowl!
How charmingly sweet you sing!
O let us be married! too long we
have tarried:
But what shall we do for a ring?'
They sailed away, for a year and a day,
To the land where the Bong-tree grows,
And there in a wood a Piggy-wig stood,
With a ring at the end of his nose,
  His nose,
  His nose,
With a ring at the end of his nose.

'Dear Pig, are you willing to sell for one
shilling
Your ring?' Said the Piggy, 'I will.'
So they took it away, and were married
next day
By the Turkey who lives on the hill.
They dined on mince, and slices of quince,
Which they ate with a runcible spoon;
And hand in hand, on the edge of the sand,
They danced by the light of the moon,
  The moon,
  The moon,
They danced by the light of the moon.

Edward Lear 1812–1888

A Wise Old Owl

A wise old owl
Lived in an oak;
The more he saw
The less he spoke.
The less he spoke
The more he heard.
Why can't we all be
Like the wise old bird?

Traditional

A Song About Myself

There was a naughty boy,
A naughty boy was he,
He would not stop at home,
He could not quiet be –
He took
In his knapsack
A book
Full of vowels
And a shirt
With some towels –
A slight cap
For night cap –
A hair brush,
Comb ditto,
New stockings
For old ones
Would split O!
This knapsack
Tight at's back
He rivetted close
And followed his nose
To the North,
To the North,
And followed
his nose
To the North.

There was a naughty boy
And a naughty boy was he,
For nothing would he do
But scribble poetry –
He took
An ink stand
In his hand
And a pen
Big as ten
In the other
And away
In a Pother
He ran
To the mountains
And fountains
And ghostès
And postès
And witches
And ditches,
And wrote
In his coat
When the weather
Was cool –

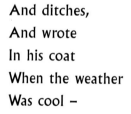

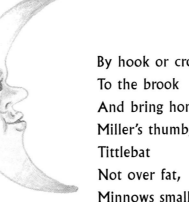

Fear of gout –
And without
When the weather
Was warm.
Och, the charm
When we choose
To follow one's nose
To the North,
To the North,
To follow one's nose
To the North!

There was a naughty boy
And a naughty boy was he,
He kept little fishes
In washing tubs three
In spite
Of the might
Of the maid
Nor afraid
Of his Granny good,
He often would
Hurly burly
Get up early
And go,

By hook or crook,
To the brook
And bring home
Miller's thumb,
Tittlebat
Not over fat,
Minnows small
As the stall
Of a glove,
Not above
The size
Of a nice
Little baby's
Little fingers –
O he made
('Twas his trade)
Of fish a pretty kettle
A kettle –
A kettle,
Of fish a pretty
kettle,
A kettle!

There was a naughty boy,
And a naughty boy was he,
He ran away to Scotland
The people for to see –
Then he found
That the ground
Was as hard,
That a yard
Was as long,
That a song
Was as merry,
That a cherry
Was as red,
That lead
Was as weighty,
That fourscore
Was as eighty,
That a door
Was as wooden
As in England –
So he stood in his shoes
And he wondered,
He wondered,
He stood in his shoes
And he wondered.

John Keats 1795–1821

Summer is Gone

I have but one story –
The stags are moaning,
The sky is snowing,
Summer is gone.

Quickly the low sun
Goes drifting down
Behind the rollers,
Lifting and long.

The wild geese cry
Down the storm;
The ferns have fallen,
Russet and torn.

The wings of the birds
Are clotted with ice
I have but one story –
Summer is gone.

Anonymous

The Quangle Wangle's Hat

On the top of the
Crumpetty Tree
The Quangle Wangle sat,
But his face
you could not see,
On account of his
Beaver Hat.

For his Hat was
a hundred and two feet wide,
With ribbons and bibbons
on every side
And bells, and buttons,
and loops, and lace,
So that nobody ever
could see the face
Of the Quangle Wangle Quee.

The Quangle Wangle said
To himself on the
Crumpetty Tree, –
'Jam and jelly; and bread;

Are the best food for me!
But the longer I live
on this Crumpetty Tree,
The plainer than ever
it seems to me

That very few people
come this way,
And that life on the whole
is far from gay!'
Said the Quangle
Wangle Quee.

But there came to the
Crumpetty Tree,
Mr and Mrs Canary;
And they said, –
'Did you ever see
Any spot so charmingly airy?'

'May we build a nest
on your lovely Hat?
Mr Quangle Wangle,
grant us that!
O please let us come
and build a nest
Of whatever material
suits you best,
Mr Quangle Wangle Quee!'

And besides, to the
Crumpetty Tree
Came the Stork, the Duck,
and the Owl;
The Snail, and the
Bumble-Bee,
The Frog, and the
Fimble Fowl;

The Fimble Fowl, with a
Corkscrew leg;
And all of them said, –
'We humbly beg,
We may build our homes
on your lovely Hat, –
Mr Quangle Wangle,
grant us that!
Mr Quangle Wangle Quee!'

And the Golden grouse
came there
And the Pobble who
has no toes, –
And the small
Olympian bear, –
And the Dong with
a luminous nose.

And the Blue Baboon,
who played the flute, –
And the Orient Calf
from the Land of Tute, –
And the Attery Squash,
and the Bisky Bat, –
All came and built
on the lovely Hat
Of the Quangle Wangle Quee.

And the Quangle Wangle said
To himself on the
Crumpetty Tree, –
'When all these
creatures move
What a wonderful
noise there'll be!'

And at night by the light
of the Mulberry moon,
They danced to the Flute
of the Blue Baboon,
On the broad green leaves
of the Crumpetty Tree,
And all were as happy
as happy could be
With the Quangle
Wangle Quee.

Edward Lear 1812–1888

David and Goliath

When Israel against Philistia
War waged under Saul,
A giant in their host they saw,
Whom they Goliath call.

In height he others did surpass,
In strength he did excel;
He had a head-piece all of brass,
And he with pride did swell.

Who marching to their tents doth boast
And insolently cry,
With the best captains in their host
His courage he will try.

The Israelites were in great fear,
And trembling at his voice,
Which made their enemies scoff and jeer,
And over them rejoice.

Thus proud Goliath oft doth vaunt,
And challenge them to fight,
But Israel's generals courage want,
To meet this man of might.

When David came into the host,
And heard his blasphemies,
Displeased he should thus huff and boast
'I'll fight with him,' he cries.

Goliath does this youth despise,
Swears he will have his life;
David as valiantly replies,
His death shall end the strife.

Goliath came with sword and spear,
But David with a sling;
And though the giant rage and swear,
Down David doth him bring.

He only slings a little stone,
And therewith lays him dead;
Which done, he bravely marches on,
And then cuts off his head.

Nathaniel Crouch 1632–1725

Whether the Weather be Fine

Whether the weather be fine
Or whether the weather be not,
Whether the weather be cold
Or whether the weather be hot,
We'll weather the weather
Whatever the weather,
Whether we like it or not.

Anonymous

70

O hark, O hear! how thin and clear,
 And thinner, clearer, farther going!
O sweet and far from cliff and scar
The horns of Elfland faintly blowing!
Blow, let us hear the purple glens replying:
Blow, bugle; answer, echoes, dying, dying,
dying.

Blow, Bugle, Blow

The splendour falls on castle walls
And snowy summits old in story:
The long light shakes across the lakes,
And the wild cataract leaps in glory.
Blow, bugle, blow, set the wild echoes flying,
Blow, bugle, answer, echoes, dying, dying,
dying.

O love, they die in yon rich sky,
They faint on hill or field or river:
Our echoes roll from soul to soul,
And grow for ever and for ever.
Blow, bugle, blow, set the wild
echoes flying,
And answer, echoes, answer,
dying, dying, dying.

Alfred, Lord Tennyson 1809–1892

Monday's Child

Monday's child is fair of face,
Tuesday's child is full of grace,
Wednesday's child is full of woe,
Thursday's child has far to go,
Friday's child is loving and giving,
Saturday's child works hard for his living,
And the child that is born on the
Sabbath day
Is bonny and blithe, and good and gay.

Anonymous

Star Light, Star Bright

Star light, star bright
First star I see tonight,
I wish I may, I wish I might,
Have the wish I wish tonight.

Anonymous

A Child's Thought

At seven, when I go to bed,
I find such pictures in my head:
Castles with dragons prowling round,
Gardens where magic fruits are found;
Fair ladies prisoned in a tower,
Or lost in an enchanted bower;
While gallant horsemen ride by streams
That border all this land of dreams
I find, so clearly in my head
At seven, when I go to bed.

Robert Louis Stevenson
1850–1894

Travel

I should like to rise and go
Where the golden apples grow;
Where below another sky
Parrot islands anchored lie,
And, watched by cockatoos and goats,
Lonely Crusoes building boats;
Where in sunshine reaching out
Eastern cities, miles about,
Are with mosque and minaret
Among sandy gardens set,
And the rich goods from near and far
Hang for sale in the bazaar;
Where the Great Wall round China goes,
And on one side the desert blows,
And with bell and voice and drum,
Cities on the other hum;

Where are forests, hot as fire,
Wide as England, tall as a spire,
Full of apes and coco-nuts
And the negro hunters' huts;
Where the knotty crocodile
Lies and blinks in the Nile,
And the red flamingo flies
Hunting fish before his eyes;
Where in jungles, near and far,
Man-devouring tigers are,
Lying close and giving ear
Lest the hunt be drawing near,
Or a comer-by be seen
Swinging in a palanquin;
Where among the desert sands
Some deserted city stands

All its children, sweep and prince,
Grown to manhood ages since,
Not a foot in street or house,
Not a stir of child or mouse,
And when kindly falls the night,
In all the town no spark of light.
There I'll come when I'm a man
With a camel caravan;
Light a fire in the gloom
Of some dusty dining-room;
See the pictures on the walls,
Heroes, fights and festivals;
And in a corner find the toys
Of the old Egyptian boys.

Robert Louis Stevenson 1850–1894

Swing, Swing

Swing, swing,
Sing, sing,
Here! my throne and I am king!
Swing, swing,
Sing, sing,
Farewell, earth, for I'm on the wing!

Low, high,
Here I fly,
Like a bird through sunny sky;
Free, free,
Over the lea,
Over the mountain, over the sea!

Soon, soon,
Afternoon,
Over the sunset, over the moon;
Far, far,
Over all bar,
Sweeping on from star to star!

No, no,
Low, low,
Sweeping daisies with my toe.
Slow, slow,
To and fro,
Slow – slow – slow – slow.

William Allingham 1824—1889

Cuckoo

Cuckoo, cuckoo
What do you do?
In April,
I open my bill;
In May,
I sing night and day;
In June,
I change my tune;
In July,
Away I fly;
In August,
Go I must.

Anonymous

Hush Little Baby

Hush little baby, don't say a word,
Papa's going to buy you a mockingbird.

If that mockingbird won't sing,
Papa's going to buy you a diamond ring.

If that diamond ring turns brass,
Papa's going to buy you a looking glass.

If that looking glass gets broke,
Papa's going to buy you a billy goat.

If that billy goat won't pull,
Papa's going to buy you a cart and bull.

If that cart and bull fall down,
You'll still be the sweetest little baby in town.

Anonymous

Five Little Chickens

Said the first little chicken,
With a queer little squirm,
'Oh, I wish I could find
A fat little worm!'

Said the next little chicken,
With an odd little shrug,
'Oh, I wish I could find
A fat little bug!'

Said the third little chicken,
With a sharp little squeal,
'Oh, I wish I could find
Some nice yellow meal!'

Said the fourth little chicken,
With a small sigh of grief,
'Oh, I wish I could find
A green little leaf!'

Said the fifth little chicken,
With a faint little moan,
'Oh, I wish I could find
A wee gravel stone!'

'Now, see here,' said the mother,
From the green garden-patch,
'If you want any breakfast,
You must come here and scratch.'

Anonymous

The Sea-gull

The waves leap up, the wild wind blows,
And the Gulls together crowd,
And wheel about, and madly scream
To the deep sea roaring loud.
And let the sea roar ever so loud,
And the wind pipe ever so high,
With a wilder joy the bold Sea-gull
Sends forth a wilder cry.

For the Sea-gull, he is a daring bird,
And he loves with the storm to sail;
To ride in the strength of the billowy sea,
And to breast the driving gale!
The little boat, she is tossed about,
Like a sea-weed, to and fro;
The tall ship reels like a drunken man,
As the gusty tempests blow.

But the Sea-gull
laughs at the
fear of man,
And sails in a wild delight
On the torn-up breast of the night-black sea,
Like a foam cloud, calm and white.
The waves may rage and the winds may roar,
But he fears not wreck nor need;
For he rides the sea, in its stormy strength,
As a strong man rides his steed.

Oh, the white Sea-gull, the bold Sea-gull!
He makes on the shore his nest,
And he tries what the inland fields may be;
But he loveth the sea the best!
And away from land a thousand leagues,
He goes 'mid surging foam;
What matter to him is land or shore,
For the sea is his truest home!

Mary Howitt 1799–1888

The Swallow

Fly away, fly away, over the sea,
Sun-loving swallow, for summer is done.
Come again, come again, come back to me,
Bring the summer and bring the sun.

Christina Rossetti
1830–1894

The Parrot

I am the pirate's parrot,
I sail the seven seas
And sleep inside the crow's nest.
Don't look for me in trees!

I am the pirate's parrot,
A bird both brave and bold.
I guard the captain's treasure
And count his hoard of gold.

Anonymous

The Tyger

Tyger! Tyger! burning bright
In the forests of the night,
What immortal hand or eye
Could frame thy fearful symmetry?

In what distant deeps or skies
Burnt the fire of thine eyes?
On what wings dare he aspire?
What the hand dare seize the fire?

And what shoulder, and what art,
Could twist the sinews of thy heart?
And when thy heart began to beat,
What dread hand? and what dread feet?

What the hammer? what the chain?
In what furnace was thy brain?
What the anvil? what dread grasp
Dare its deadly terrors clasp?

When the stars threw down their spears,
And water'd heaven with their tears,
Did he smile his work to see?
Did he who made the Lamb make thee?

Tyger! Tyger! burning bright
In the forests of the night,
What immortal hand or eye
Dare frame thy fearful symmetry?

William Blake 1757–1827

What are Heavy?

What are heavy? Sea-sand and sorrow;
What are brief? Today and tomorrow;
What are frail? Spring blossoms and youth;
What are deep? The ocean and truth.

Christina Rossetti 1830–1894

A Warning

The robin and the redbreast,
The robin and the wren,
If you take them from their nests,
Ye'll ne'er thrive again.

The robin and the redbreast,
The martin and the swallow,
If you touch one of their eggs,
Ill luck is sure to follow.

Anonymous

Ladybird, Ladybird

Ladybird, ladybird, fly away home;
The house is on fire, thy children all gone –
All but one, and her name is Ann,
And she crept under a pudding-pan.

Anonymous

Trees

The Oak is called the king of trees,
The Aspen quivers in the breeze,
The Poplar grows up straight and tall,
The Peach tree spreads along the wall,
The Sycamore gives pleasant shade,
The Willow droops in watery glade,
The Fir tree useful timber gives,
The Beech amid the forest lives.

Sara Coleridge 1802–1852

Grey Goose and Gander

Grey goose and gander,
Weft your wings together,
And carry the King's fair daughter
Over the one-strand river.

Traditional

Cock Robin

Who killed Cock Robin?
'I,' said the Sparrow,
'With my bow and arrow,
I killed Cock Robin.'

Who saw him die?
'I,' said the Fly,
'With my little eye,
I saw him die.'

Who caught his blood?
'I,' said the Fish,
'With my little dish,
I caught his blood.'

Who'll make his shroud?
'I,' said the Beetle,
'With my thread and needle,
I'll make his shroud.'

Who'll dig his grave?
'I,' said the Owl,
'With my spade and trowel,
I'll dig his grave.'

Who'll be the parson?
'I,' said the Rook,
'With my little book,
I'll be the parson.'

Who'll be the clerk?
'I,' said the Lark,
'I'll say Amen in the dark;
I'll be the clerk.'

Who'll be chief mourner?
'I,' said the Dove,
'I mourn for my love;
I'll be chief mourner.'

Who'll bear the torch?
'I,' said the Linnet,
'I'll come in a minute,
I'll bear the torch.'

Who'll sing his dirge?
'I,' said the Thrush,
'As I sing in the bush
I"ll sing his dirge.'

Who'll bear the pall?
'We,' said the Wren,
Both the Cock and the Hen;
'We'll bear the pall.'

Who'll carry his coffin?
'I,' said the Kite,
'If it be in the night,
I'll carry his coffin.'

Who'll toll the bell?
'I,' said the Bull,
'Because I can pull,
I'll toll the bell.'

All the birds of the air
Fell to sighing and sobbing
When they heard the bell toll
For poor Cock Robin.

Anonymous

The North Wind Doth Blow

The north wind doth blow,
And we shall have snow,
And what will poor robin do then,
Poor thing?

He'll sit in a barn,
And keep himself warm,
And hide his head under his wing,
Poor thing.

Anonymous

'Don't-Care Didn't Care'

Don't-care didn't care;
Don't-care was wild.
Don't-care stole plum and pear
Like any beggar's child.

Don't-care was made to care,
Don't-care was hung:
Don't-care was put in the pot
And boiled till he was done.

Traditional

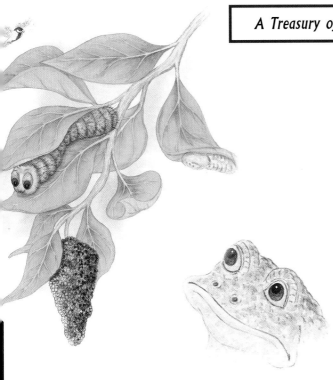

The Wind

Who has seen the wind?
Neither I nor you;
But when the leaves hang trembling
The wind is passing through.

Who has seen the wind?
Neither you nor I;
But when the trees bow down their heads
The wind is passing by.

Anonymous

Caterpillar

Brown and furry
Caterpillar in a hurry,
Take your walk
To the shady leaf, or stalk,
Or what not,
Which may be the chosen spot.
No toad spy you,
Hovering bird of prey pass by you;
Spin and die,
To live again a butterfly.

Anonymous

Beasts and Birds

The dog will come when he is called,
The cat will walk away;
The monkey's cheek is very bald,
The goat is fond of play.
The parrot is a prate – apace,
Yet knows not what she says;
The noble horse will win the race,
Or draw you in a chaise.

The pig is not a feeder nice,
The squirrel loves a nut,
The wolf would eat you in a trice,
The buzzard's eyes are shut.
The lark sings high up in the air,
The linnet in the tree;
The swan he has a bosom fair,
And who so proud as he?

Adelaide O'Keefe 1776–1855

King Arthur

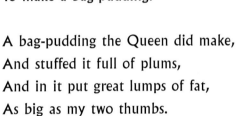

When Good King
Arthur ruled the land,
He was a goodly king;
He stole three pecks of
barley-meal,
To make a bag-pudding.

A bag-pudding the Queen did make,
And stuffed it full of plums,
And in it put great lumps of fat,
As big as my two thumbs.

The King and Queen sat down to dine,
And all the court beside;
And what they could not eat that night,
The Queen next morning fried.

Traditional

Where the hazel
bank is steepest,
Where the shadow
falls the deepest,
Where the clustering
nuts fall free,
That's the way for Billy and me.

A Boy's Song

Where the pools are bright and deep,
Where the grey trout lies asleep,
Up the river and o'er the lea,
That's the way for Billy and me.

Where the blackbird sings the latest,
Where the hawthorn blooms the sweetest,
Where the nestlings chirp and flee,
That's the way for Billy and me.

Where the mowers mow the cleanest,
Where the hay lies thick and greenest;
There to trace the homeward bee,
That's the way for Billy and me.

Why the boys should drive away
Little sweet maidens from the play,
Or love to banter and fight so well,
That's the thing I never could tell.

But this I know, I love to play,
Through the meadow, among the hay,
Up the water and o'er the lea,
That's the way for Billy and me.

James Hogg 1770–1835

The Cataract of Lodore

'How does the Water
Come down at Lodore?'
My little boy asked me
Thus, once on a time;
And moreover he tasked me
To tell him in rhyme.
Anon at the word,
There first came one daughter
And then came another,
To second and third
The request of their brother
And to hear how the water
Comes down at Lodore,
With its rush and its roar,
As many a time
They had seen it before.
So I told them in rhyme,
And 'twas in my vocation
For their recreation
That so I should sing;
Because I was Laureate
To them and the King.

From its sources which well
In the Tarn on the fell;
From its fountains
In the mountains
Its rills and its gills;
Through moss and through brake,
It runs and it creeps
For awhile, till it sleeps

In its own little lake.
And thence at departing,
Awakening and starting,
It runs through the reeds
And away it proceeds,

Through meadow and glade,
In sun and in shade,
And through the wood-shelter,
Among crags in its flurry,
Helter-skelter,
Hurry-scurry.
Here it comes sparkling,
And there it lies darkling;
Now smoking and
frothing
Its tumult and
wrath in,
Till in this rapid race
On which it is bent
It reaches the place
Of its steep descent.

The Cataract strong
Then plunges along,
Striking and raging
As if a war waging
Its caverns and rocks
among:
Rising and leaping,
Sinking and creeping,
Swelling and sweeping,
Showering and springing,
Flying and flinging,
Writhing and ringing,
Eddying and whisking,
Spouting and frisking,
Turning and twisting,
Around and around
With endless rebound!
Smiting and fighting,

A sight to delight in;
Confounding, astounding,
Dizzying and deafening the ear with its
sound.
Collecting, projecting,
Receding and speeding,
And shocking and rocking,
And darting and parting,
And threading and spreading,
And whizzing and hissing,
And dripping and skipping,
And hitting and splitting,
And shining and twining,
And rattling and battling,
And shaking and quaking,
And pouring and roaring,
And waving and raving,
And tossing and crossing,
And flowing and going,
And running and stunning,
And foaming and roaming,
And dinning and spinning,
And dropping and hopping,
And working and jerking,
And guggling and struggling,
And heaving and cleaving,
And moaning and groaning;
And glittering and frittering,
And gathering and feathering,

And whitening and brightening,
And quivering and shivering,
And hurrying and scurrying,
And thundering and floundering;
Dividing and gliding and sliding,
And falling and brawling and sprawling,
And driving and riving and striving,
And sprinkling and twinkling and wrinkling,
And sounding and bounding and rounding,
And bubbling and troubling and doubling,
And grumbling and rumbling and tumbling,
   And clattering and battering and
     shattering;
      Retreating and beating and meeting
       and sheeting,
       Delaying and straying and playing
       and spraying,
       Advancing and prancing and
       glancing and dancing,
        Recoiling, turmoiling and toiling
        and boiling,

And gleaming
and streaming
and steaming and
beaming,
And rushing and
flushing and
brushing and
gushing,
And flapping and rapping and clapping and
slapping,
And curling and whirling and purling
and twirling,
And thumping and plumping and
bumping and jumping,
And dashing and flashing and splashing
and clashing;
And so never ending, but always
descending,
Sounds and motions for ever and ever
are blending,
All at once and all o'er, with a
mighty uproar,
And this way the water comes down
at Lodore.

Robert Southey 1744–1843

Oranges and Lemons

Oranges and lemons,
Say the bells of
St. Clement's.

You owe me five farthings,
Say the bells of St. Martin's.

When will you pay me?
Say the bells of Old Bailey.

When I grow rich,
Say the bells of Shoreditch.

When will that be?
Say the bells of Stepney.
I'm sure I don't know,
Says the great bell of Bow.

Traditional

Hurt No Living Thing

Hurt no living thing;
Ladybird, nor butterfly,
Nor moth with dusty wing,
Nor cricket chirping cheerily,
Nor grasshopper so light of leap,
Nor dancing gnat, nor beetle fat,
Nor harmless little worms that creep.

Christina Rossetti
1830–1894

As I was Going to St Ives

As I was going to St Ives,
I met a man with seven wives;
Each wife had seven sacks,
Each sack had seven cats,
Each cat had seven kits:
Kits, cats, sacks, wives,
How many were going
To St Ives?

Anonymous